A Beginner's Guide to

MICROSOFT POWERPOINT
For the Elderly

An Illustrative Step-by-Step Guide to
Learning PowerPoint for Senior Citizens

THOMAS JACKSON

Copyright

Thomas Jackson
Olasis Publishing House
USA | UK | Canada
© Olasis Publishing House 2020

Printed in the United States of America
©2020 by Thomas Jackson

About the Author

Thomas Jackson is a tech enthusiast with about 10 years' experience in the ICT industry. He is passionate about the latest technical and technological trends. Thomas holds a Bachelor and a master's degree in Computer Science and Information Communication Technology respectively from MIT, Boston Massachusetts.

Table of Contents

INTRODUCTION

A Beginner's Guide to PowerPoint covers all you would need to successfully create presentations with PowerPoint. Starting from the basics, you learn how to create, edit, format your slides. You will also learn how to apply themes, change background color, and how to add charts to your slides.

This book is concise and to the point as you do not need to wade through a wall of text to learn how to quickly carry out a task in PowerPoint. Thus, you will not see the unnecessary verbosity and filler text you may find in some other PowerPoint books in this book. The aim is to take even a complete newbie to someone that is skilled in PowerPoint within a few hours.

Who Is This Book For?

Beginner's Guide to PowerPoint starts from the basics so it is suitable for you if you are new to PowerPoint. This book is also for you if you have some skills in PowerPoint and you are looking to expand on it by learning the new features in PowerPoint 2019.

The necessary topics have been covered to give you a solid foundation. However, the topics have been kept at a level not to be overwhelming to someone completely new to PowerPoint and interested in a quick course without getting bored with the more advance topics.

This book is aimed at readers with Microsoft PowerPoint 2019, however, many of the core features remain the same for earlier versions of the software like PowerPoint 2016, 2013, and 2010. You would still find many of the lessons in this book to be relevant irrespective of the PowerPoint version you have.

How to Use This Book

This guide can be used as a step-by-step training guide as well as a reference manual that you come back to from time to time. You can read it from start to finish or skip to certain parts that covers the topics you want to learn. Even though the chapters are organized in a logical manner, it has been designed to enable you read a chapter as a standalone tutorial to learn how to do certain things.

There are different ways to carry out some task in PowerPoint, so, for brevity, I have focused on the most effective way of carrying out a task. On few occasions I also provided alternative ways to carry out a task.

Assumptions

The software and hardware assumptions made when writing this book is that you already have PowerPoint 2019 installed on your computer and that you are working on the Windows 10 platform.

GETTING STARTED

There are different ways to launch Microsoft PowerPoint on Windows 10. To begin, click on the Windows start menu on your computer screen or the Windows button on your keyboard. The programs are sorted out in alphabetic order, scroll down to the group of programs starting with P. You'll see PowerPoint as part of the list.

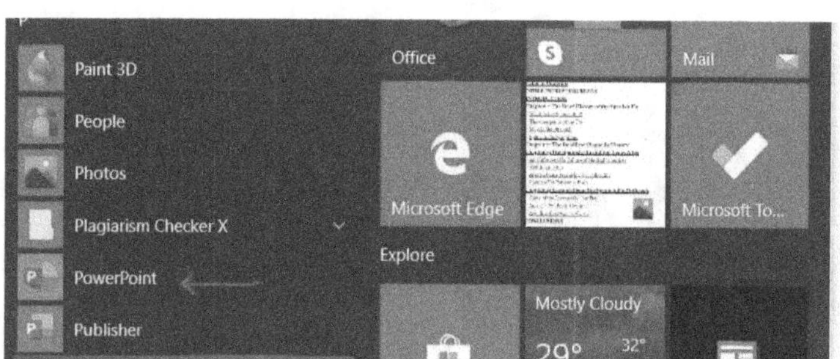

Alternatively, there are other ways you can be able to access PowerPoint faster next time when you want to make use of it. You can pin it to the Start menu, pin to taskbar, or create a desktop shortcut.

To pin PowerPoint to your Start menu:

1. Click on the Windows Start menu.

2. Scroll down to the group of applications under P.

3. Right-click PowerPoint and select Pin to Start.

To pin PowerPoint to your taskbar:

1. Click on the Start menu.

2. Scroll down to the group of programs starting with P.

3. Right-click PowerPoint and click on "More" and "Pin to taskbar."

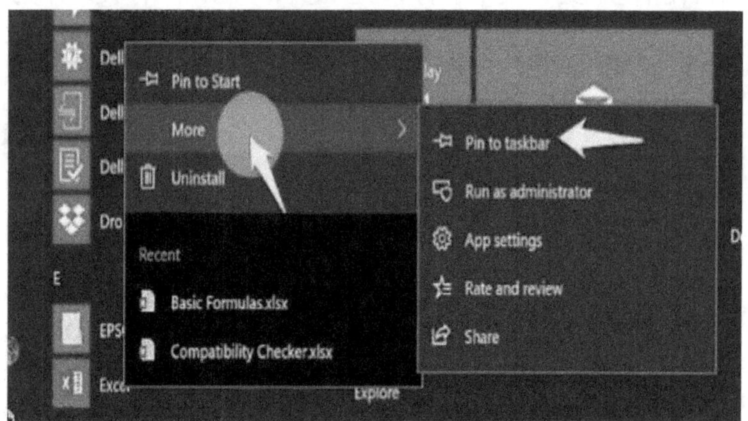

To Create a desktop shortcut:

1. Click on the Start menu.

2. Right-click PowerPoint and click on "More" and then on "Open file location". This will open the shortcut folder location of PowerPoint.

3. In the folder, right-click on PowerPoint and click on Copy.

4. On your desktop, right-click any area and select paste.

5. To open the Microsoft PowerPoint from its desktop shortcut. You have to Double-click on the PowerPoint shortcut icon.

Creating a New PowerPoint Presentation

On opening PowerPoint, it will display its Home screen. The start screen enables you to create a blank presentation or open a recent PowerPoint presentation. You can also select a predefined template according to what you would be using your presentation for.

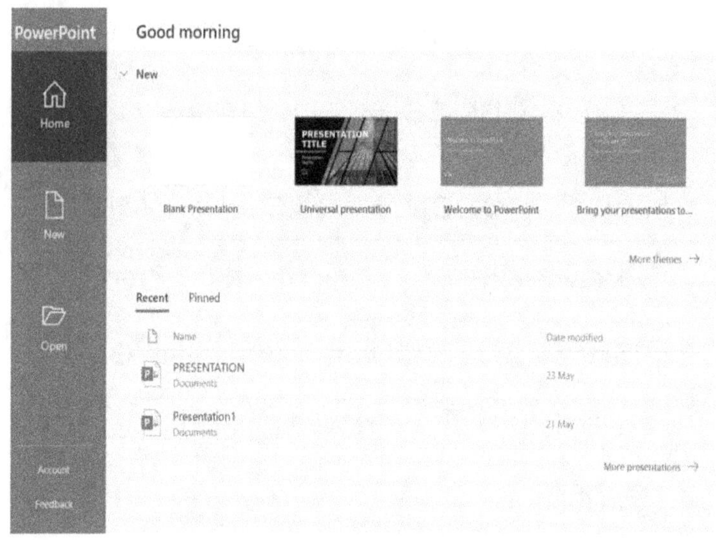

To create a PowerPoint file, click on "Blank presentation". A new presentation named **Presentation1** would be created.

Note: You can create a new presentation quickly when you already have one opened by pressing **CTRL + N** on your keyboard.

Saving a PowerPoint Presentation

It is a good practice to save your presentation the first few minutes after entering data into the slide to avoid losing all your information in case something happens. There are several ways to save a presentation for the first time.

1. Firstly, click on the save icon on the Quick Access Toolbar or click on the File tab and this will open the Backstage view.

2. Click on Save As.

3. On the next display, click on This PC or OneDrive – Personal.

4. Navigate to the folder/sub-folder that you want to save the presentation in.

5. On the dialogue popup screen, enter the name of your presentation.

6. Click on the Save button to save the presentation.

Opening an Existing Presentation

Accessing recent PowerPoint files is quite straightforward. Press CTRL + O on your keyboard, it displays the Backstage view page, you will find all your recent PowerPoint presentation on the right side of the screen. Click on the file to open it.

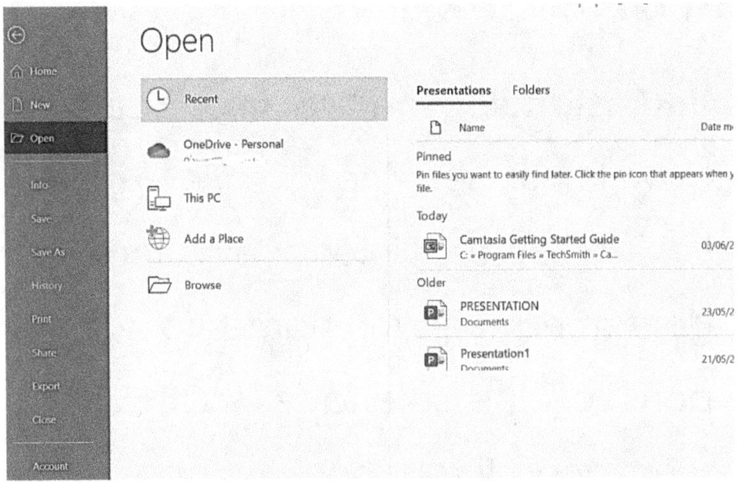

Close a Presentation

It is important to ensure that you have saved the presentation if changes where applied. To close a presentation without closing the entire PowerPoint application,

Click on File tab, the scroll down and click Close. You can also do this by using shortcut keys; simply press **CTRL + W** on your keyboard.

Understanding the User Interface

Now let us see the overview of the PowerPoint user interface so that you get familiar with the names for various parts of the interface that will be mentioned throughout this book.

Quick Access Toolbar. The Quick Access Toolbar is located at the top left corner of the screen. It is so named because this is a customizable area where you can add command for quick access.

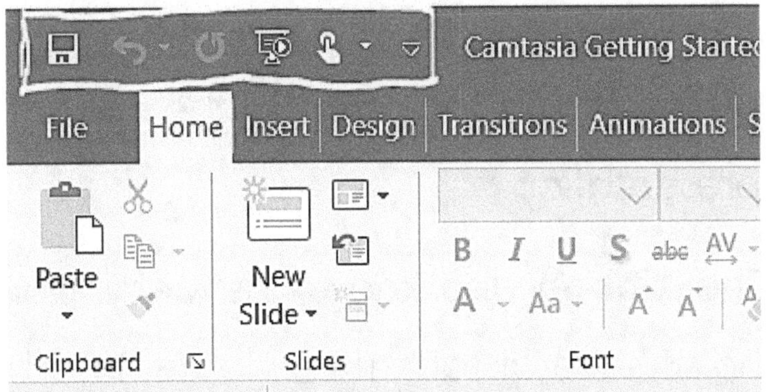

You can customize the Quick Access Toolbar to add or remove command to and from it. The steps involved in this process would be described later in this book. When you move to right from the Quick Access Toolbar, you have the title bar.

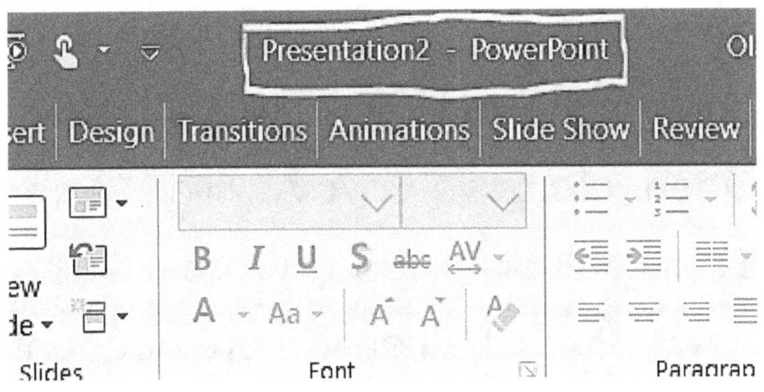

The **Title bar** displays the name of the program and the name of the current presentation.

The **Ribbon** also known as Menu bar holds several tabs (File, Home, Insert, Design, Transitions, Animations, Slide Show, Review, View, Help). These tabs hold several commands which are divided into groups for easy search for command tools.

The **File** button or tab when click on opens Backstage view, which has several options for working with your document including Home, New, Open, Info, Save, Save As, Print, Share, Export, Publish, and Close. Going down the list, there is an Account menu option where you can view user information, also there is a Feedback and Options menu.

It should be noted that if your PowerPoint presentation is saved on OneDrive, and AutoSave is enabled, the **Save As** menu option won't be available, instead you will have **Save a Copy**.

The **Home tab** provides the most used and popular set of commands like cut, copy, paste, etc. This tab contains the basic Clipboard commands, font alignment commands, style commands, commands to insert new slides.

The **Insert tab** is used when you need to insert things like a table, a diagram, a chart, a symbol, and so on into a slide.

The **Status bar** displays various information concerning the current status of an active PowerPoint slide. It also shows summary information about the range of cells selected. The information displayed on the status bar can be customized. To do this, simply right-click on the status bar and scroll down or up to change the information displayed.

To the right of the status bar are different views that are available – Normal, Slide Sorter and Reading

View. You can also find these options on the view tab. Next is the zoom feature, you can zoom in and out of your slide by sliding on the zoom tab to the right or left. Alternatively, you can zoom in or out by clicking on the plus (+) and minus (-) signs.

Customizing the Ribbon

The ribbon is the area of the screen that contains the tabs and command buttons. The ribbon is customizable, that is you can add or remove tabs and command buttons based on your preference.

To customize the ribbon, click the File tab, this displays the Backstage view. From the Backstage view, click on Options, then click on Customize Ribbon.

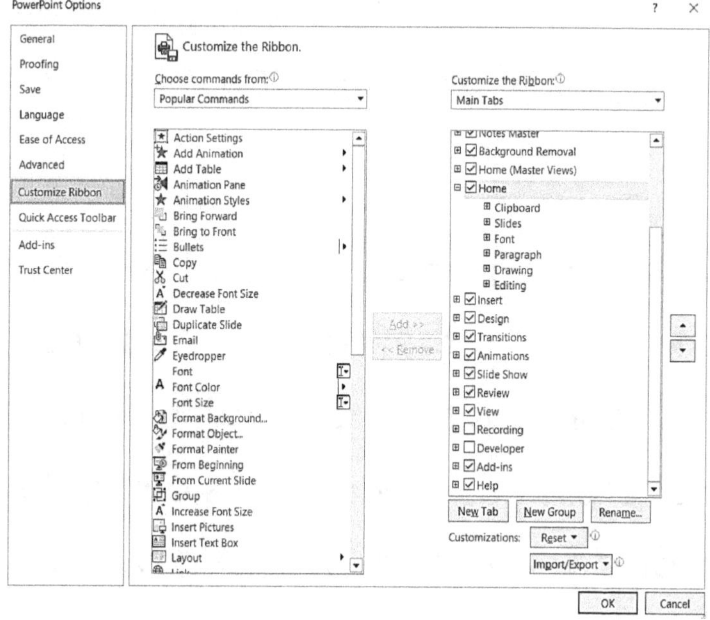

On the left side of the PowerPoint Options window, the Customize Ribbon page will be selected, and on the page, there are two main boxes. You have the command buttons that can be added to the ribbon on the left. While on the right box shows your current tabs – Main Tabs.

The group in the Main Tab box can be expanded or collapse by clicking on the plus sign (+) and minus sign (-) respectively.

Tip: It should be noted that you cannot add or remove the default commands on the ribbon, but you can hide them from the ribbon by unchecking them from the list. Also, command buttons cannot be added to default groups. To add a command button to a group, a new group must be created.

How to create a new tab:

To create a New Tab, click on the New Tab button. At least one group must be created within a tab before you can add command buttons.

How to create a group:

Select the tab (default or user created tab) in which you want to create the group. Click on the New Group button to create a new group within the tab you selected. Then select the newly created group and click on Rename to give it a name based on your preference.

How to add commands to your custom group:

1. Select your custom group in the list on the right side of the screen.

2. Select the new command button you want to add from the list on the left side of the screen.

3. Click on the Add button to add the command to the new custom group.

4. If you want to remove a command from your custom group, select the command on the right box and click on the Remove button.

5. Click on OK to confirm the change.

On viewing the customized tab on the ribbon, you will see your new group and command buttons that you added.

Customizing the Quick Access Toolbar

The Quick Access toolbar is located at the top-right corner of your PowerPoint screen. It is so named because you can easily access any command on it with a single click instead of accessing the command through the taskbar. There are several ways that command can be added to the Quick Access Toolbar. One of such ways is to click on the drop-down arrow to display a list of some of the most commonly used commands you can add to the quick access toolbar.

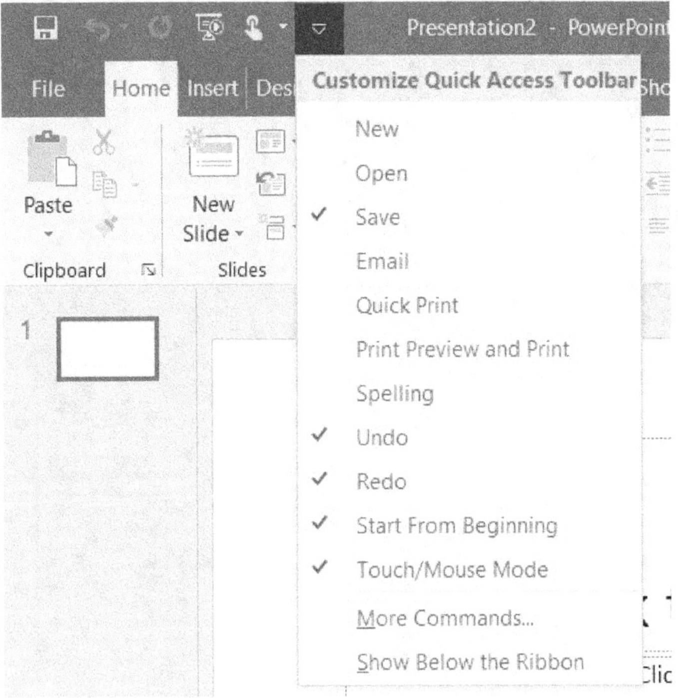

Any command you select from the drop-down menu will be added to the Quick Access Toolbar. You can have access to more options by clicking on 'More Commands' on the drop-down menu. The screen below is displayed when you click on More Commands.

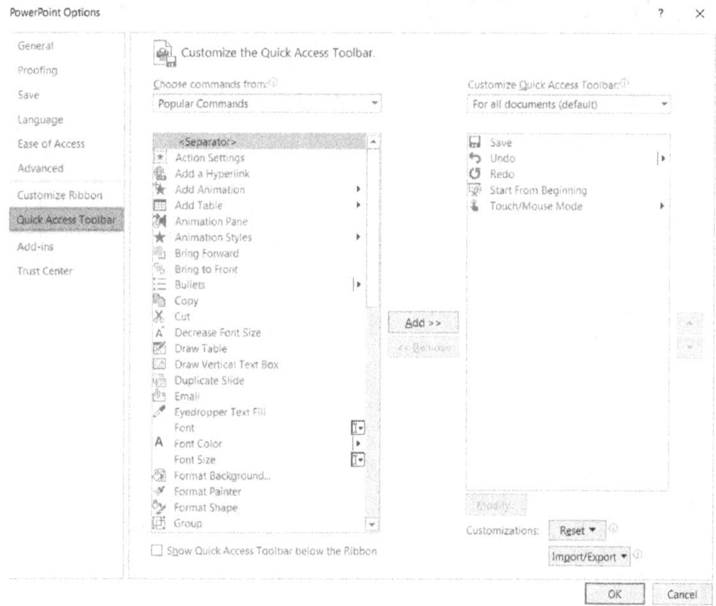

Alternatively, you can access the PowerPoint Options by Clicking the File tab, this displays the Backstage view. From the Backstage view, click on Options, then click on Quick Access Toolbar. On the left side of the PowerPoint Options window, you have the Popular commands, and the list of commands already added to the Quick Access Toolbar is on the right. To add a command from the Popular commands list to the quick access toolbar, simply click on the command and click on 'Add'.

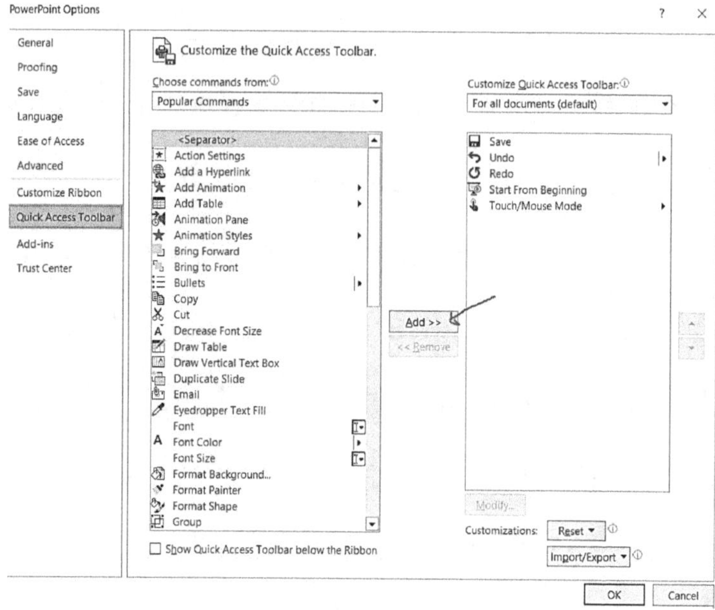

Click on the drop-down menu and select 'All Commands" if the command you wish to add to the Quick Access Toolbar is not listed under the popular commands. Scroll down to the command you wish to add, click on it and click on the Add button.

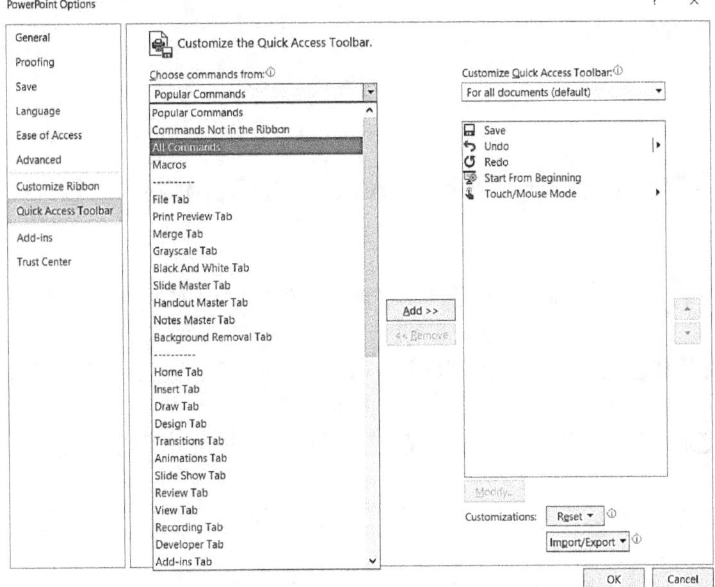

To remove a command from the Quick Access Toolbar, click on the command and then click on the Remove button.

CREATING AND MANAGING SLIDES

With PowerPoint it is easy to create attractive slides with the standard preset layouts. You can select a layout based on your preference and then add in its placeholders with text, charts or graphics.

This chapter will teach you how to design simple presentation by creating new slides. You will learn how to group slides into sections, how to rename sections in a presentation, how to apply themes etc.

How to create New Slide

From the previous chapter, you saw that when a blank presentation is created, it only has one slide.

Creating a Slide from the Slides Pane

1. In the Slide pane, click on the slide that the new slide should come after.
2. The press Enter on your keyboard. A new slide is created.

Alternatively, instead or pressing the Enter button, right click and click on New Slide. Or use the PowerPoint shortcut by pressing **CTRL + M**.

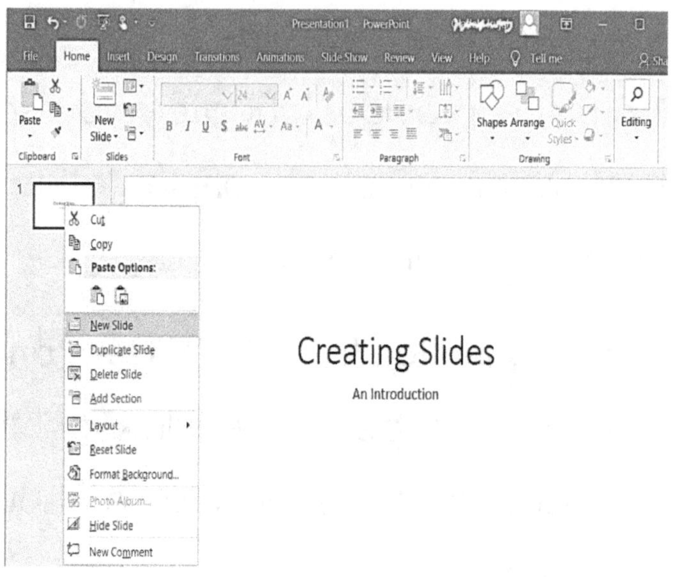

Creating a Slide from a Layout

A slide layout is a layout guide that shows PowerPoint what placeholder boxes to use on a particular slide and where to position them.

To add a slide based on slide layout:

1. Click on the slide after which you want to add the new slide.

2. On the Home tab, in the Slides group, click on the New Slide arrow to a drop-down layout menu.

3. From the drop-down menu, click on a slide layout thumbnail based on your preference to add the slide to your presentation.

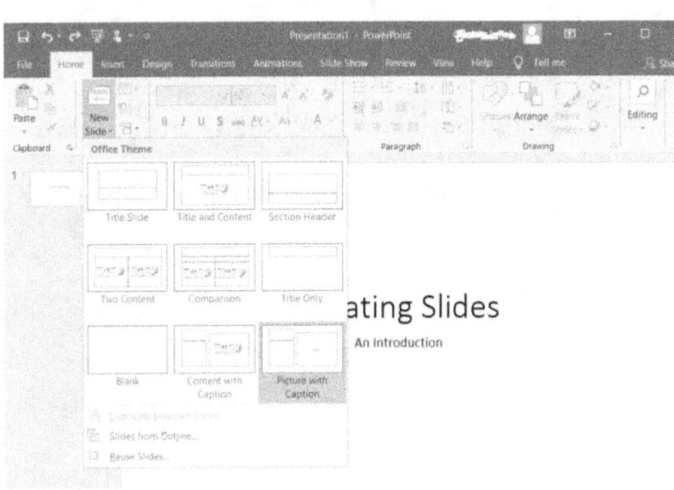

Combine slides into sections

Working with a large PowerPoint presentation can sometime make the slide pane crowded. PowerPoint has a feature that enables you to create sections that can be expanded and collapsed. This will help in making the slide pane organized, to do this:

1. In the slide pane, right-click on the slide where the section is to begin, then click on Add Section from the drop-down menu.

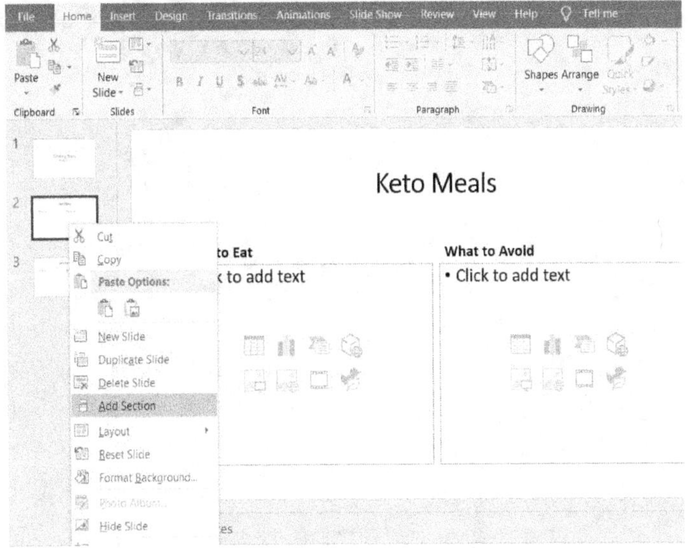

2. A dialog box opens for you to enter the name of the section. Enter the name and Click on rename button.

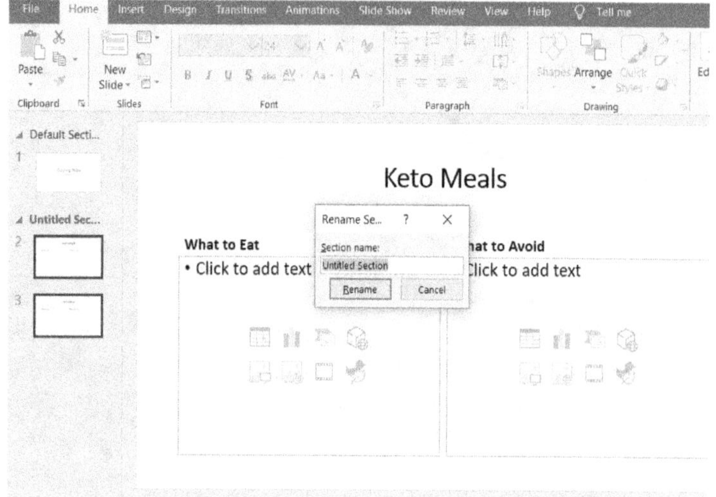

3. To shift a section, right-click on its name and use the Move Section Up and Move Section Down options.

4. To collapse or expand a certain section, click on the collapse icon to the left of the section name. You can also minimize and maximize all sections at

once by right-clicking on the section name and choosing Collapse All or Expand All.

How to rename sections

To rename section in a presentation;

1. First, right-click on the section name you wish to rename.
2. From the drop-down menu click on rename section
3. Enter the new name and click on the rename button.

How to remove a section

1. First, right-click on the section name you wish to remove.
2. Then click on Remove Section.

Hide and delete slides

How To hide or unhide slides:

- First, select the slide(s) you want to hide or unhide.
- Then right-click the selection, and then click Hide Slide. The slides that are hidden would be greyed out.

To delete slides

- Select the slide(s) you want to delete.
- Right-click the selection, and then click on Delete Slide.

Import Slides and Content

1. In the slide pane, select where in your presentation you would like the imported slide to appear

2. Click on New Slides under the HOME tab and click on Reuse Slides from the drop-down the list.

3. The Reuse Slide pane displays on the right side of the screen, then click on 'Open a PowerPoint File'.

4. From the Browse dialog pop-up, find and click on the presentation file that contains

the slide that you want to import, and then click on Open.

5. If you want the slide that you are importing to the new presentation to maintain the formatting of the original presentation, check the 'Keep source formatting' checkbox before you add the slide to the new presentation.

Also, in the Reuse Slides pane, you can do any of the following:

- Click the slide to add a single slide.

- Right-click any slide, and then click on Insert All Slides to add all of the slides.

Applying Themes

You can change the appearance of a presentation by applying themes. Microsoft PowerPoint comes with predefined themes from which you can choose from. To apply a standard theme to a presentation:

- Click on the Design tab.

- In the Themes group, click the More (bottom) arrow to display the drop-down menu that includes the Office theme gallery and any custom templates on your computer.

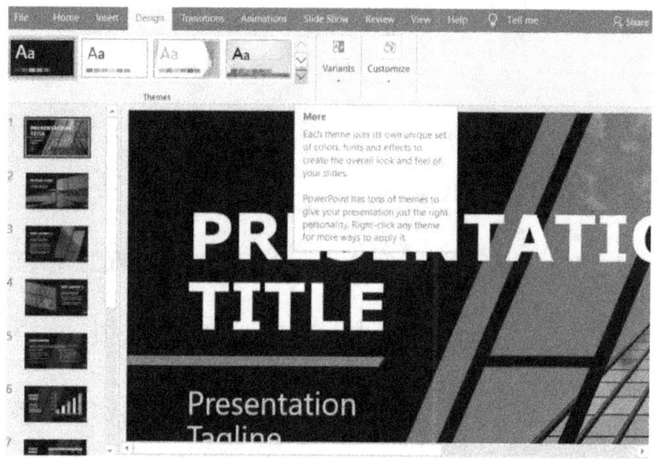

- Point the mouse cursor on the thumbnails in the gallery to display the theme names and give you a preview on the effect of applying the themes to your presentation.

- Click on a theme thumbnail that best suits your presentation to apply that theme to the entire presentation.

How to change background Color

The backgrounds of a slide are customizable, this can be done by removing background graphics and filling the slide background with a gradient color, solid color, a pattern, a texture or a picture.

- Click on the Design Tab
- Then click on Format Background

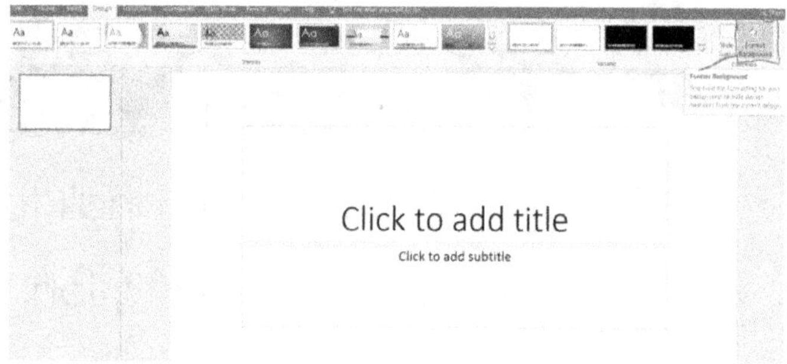

- From the Format Background pane that opens, select Solid fill or Gradient fill

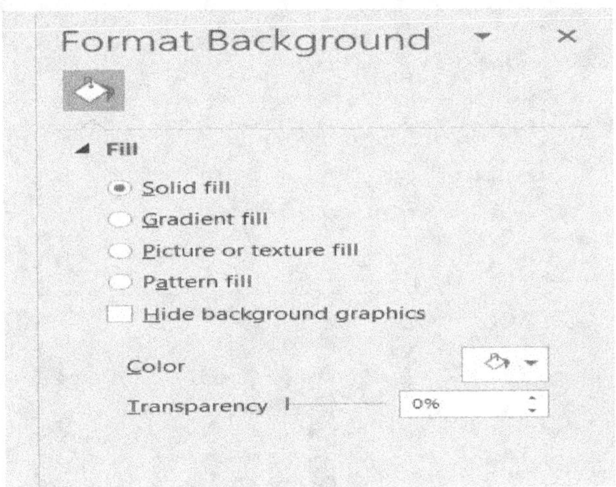

- Then select the solid or gradient color options of your choice by clicking on the Color picker.

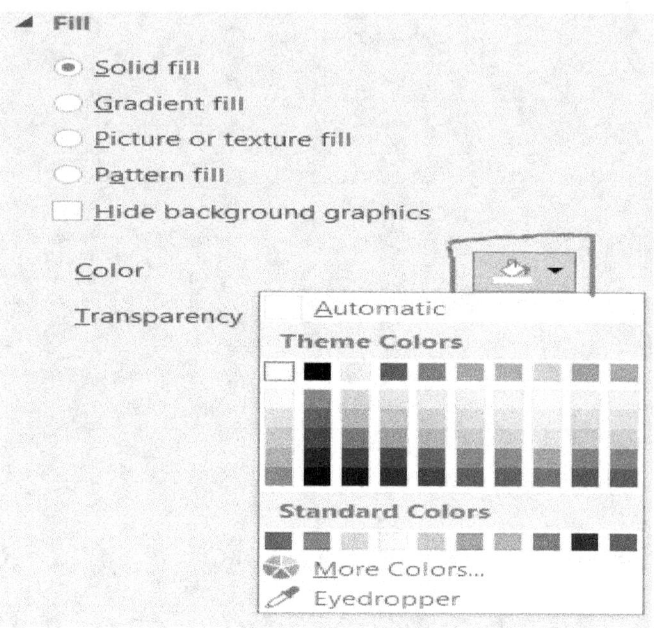

- The background color changes after selecting a color.

- Additionally, if you want to adjust transparency of the color, simply drag the Transparency slider left or right.

How to Add Slide Notes

Adding notes to each slide can help you when giving presentations. With slide notes, you can outline major points you would like to talk about. To add a note;

Simply click on Notes located on the Status bar

How to Slide Number

With PowerPoint, you can create headers and footers for your slides. The information of a header of footer includes; presentation title, slide number, and date.

- Go to the Insert Tab, then click on the Header & Footer button
- You will get a screen as shown below.

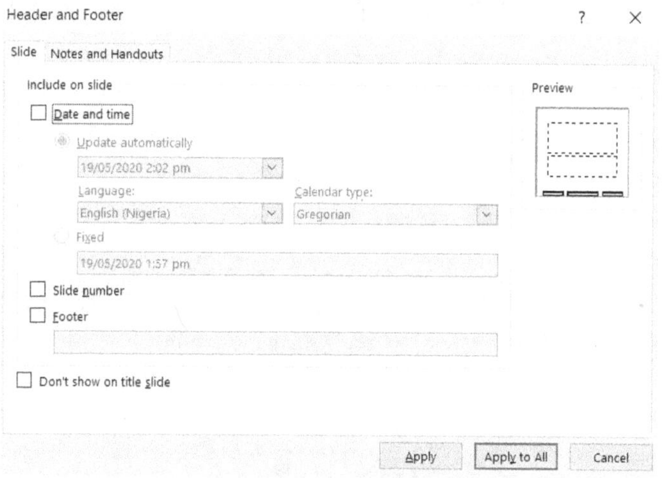

- Click on Slide number.
- Then Click on Apply to All

Note: It is a good practice to include the slide number so that it's easier for you to refer back and forth to individual slides while you present.

Rearranging Slides

- Switch to Slide Sorter view by clicking on its button.

- Choose the slide that you want to move.
- Drag the selected slide to the new location.

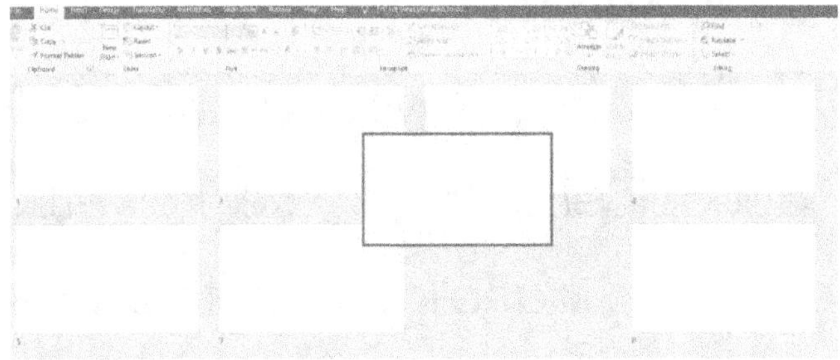

INSERT & MANAGE SLIDE CONTENTS

Text boxes (either placeholder or manual) form the basis of most presentations. Now that you know how to create them, and how to place text in them, let's take a look at how to manipulate the boxes themselves.

How to Add Text

A basic slide layout contains text placeholders, which are PowerPoint text boxes that allows you to add your own text. These might appear as empty text boxes with cues like "Click to add title". In such a case, click in these boxes and add your own text to the slide.

How Add a Text Box

To add a new text box to your slide;

- Go to the Insert Tab, then click on Text Box

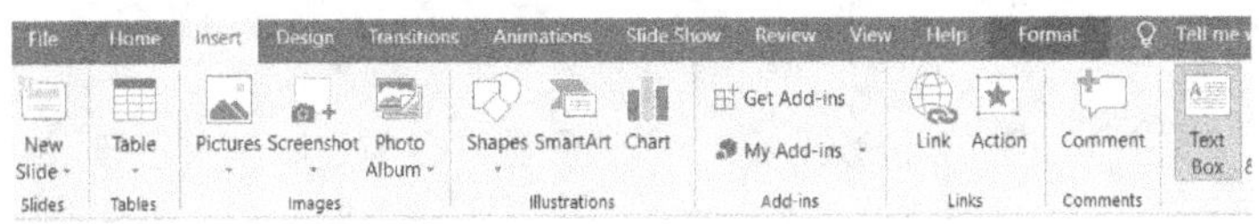

- Now click and drag on the slide where you want to insert the text box

- Once the text box is on the slide, type in it to add text to the slide.

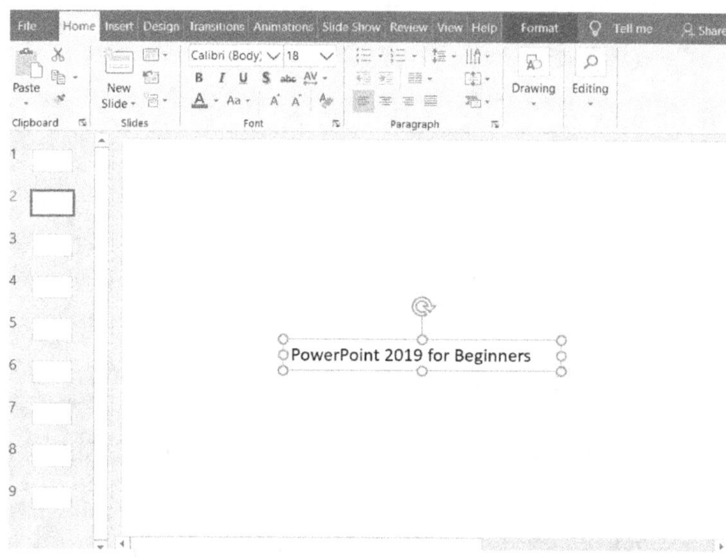

How to Change Font Appearance

Once a text is added to your slide, you can change its appearance. If you want to change the color or font of the text, simply select the text in slide and choose one of these options;

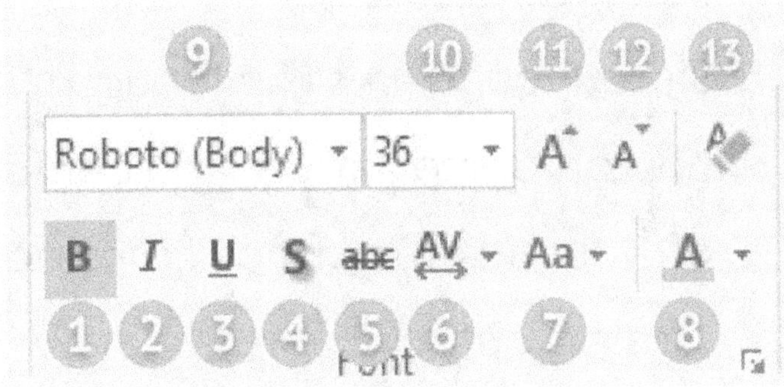

1. Bold - Use this option to make your font heavier and thicker.

2. Italic - An italic effect gives your text a bit of "lean" and is great for captions or annotations.

3. Underline - An underline is a popular tool for text headings and adds a horizontal line below your text.

4. Shadow - When your text needs contrast to stand out from the slide, add a shadow to make it more readable.

5. Strikethrough - A strikethrough is a horizontal line through the center of your text, making it appear crossed out.

6. Character Spacing - This is also sometimes called kerning, and it describes how much space is between each character in your text.

7. Change Case - This tool is a major timesaver for converting text between "cases", such as uppercase, lowercase, and

sentence case. If you have all uppercase text for example, you can change it to appear more natural.

8. Text Color - Choose from any color swatch to change the color of your text.

9. Font - Choose from different typefaces like Arial, Times New Roman, or a custom font.

10. Font Size - A higher number would show your text larger, while a smaller number decreases the text size.

11. Increase Text Size - Make your text size larger.

12.   Decrease Text Size - Make your text size smaller.

13.   Clear Formatting - Remove all of the text options you've applied to reset it.

Inserting nonstandard characters

PowerPoint has a huge array of symbols that you can insert into a slide. The types of symbols are shown below.

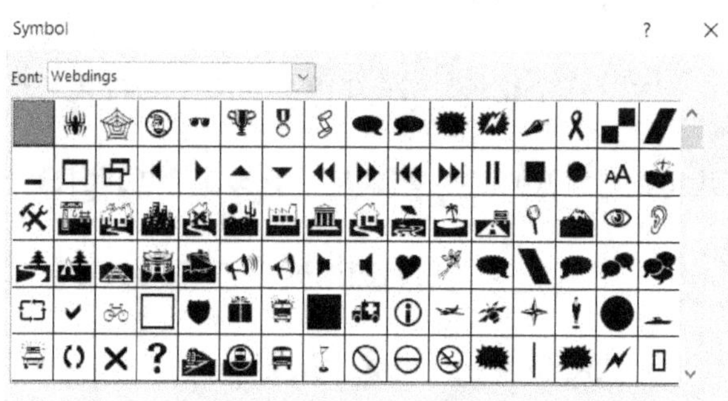

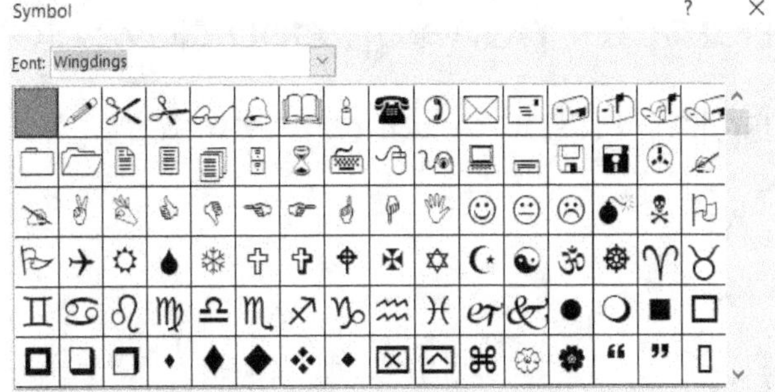

How to insert a symbol

- Click on the area where you want to insert the symbol.

- Go to the Insert tab, click on the Symbol button to open the Symbol dialog box.

- Click the font list in the dialog box, and then click on a symbol font such as **Symbol**, **Webdings**, or Wingdings to display the characters of that font. Scroll the character pane up and down to display additional characters.

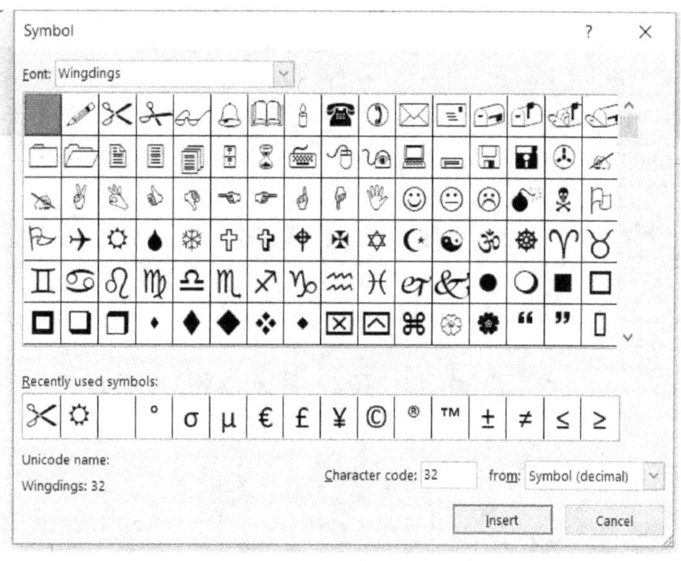

- Click the symbol you want to insert, and then click Insert.

- Then click close.

How to Add Picture

Adding pictures to your presentation can make it more interesting and engaging. To insert a picture from a file:

- Go to the Insert tab, then click on Pictures and then click on This Device from the drop-down menu.

- Locate and select your desire picture from the dialog box that appeares. Then click on Insert.
- The picture will appear on the currently selected slide.

Tip: You can also click the Pictures command in a placeholder to insert images.

Inserting online pictures

You can find a picture online to add to your presentation if you do not have the picture on your PC.

- Go to the Insert tab, then click on Online Pictures and then click on This Device from the drop-down menu.

- The Insert Pictures dialog box will appear.

- From the dialog box, you can choose between Bing Image Search or your OneDrive. In our example, we'll be making use Bing Image Search.

- Press the enter key. Your search results will appear in the dialog box.

- Select the desired image, then click Insert.

- The image will appear on the currently selected slide.

Tip: You can also click the Online Pictures command in a placeholder to insert online images.

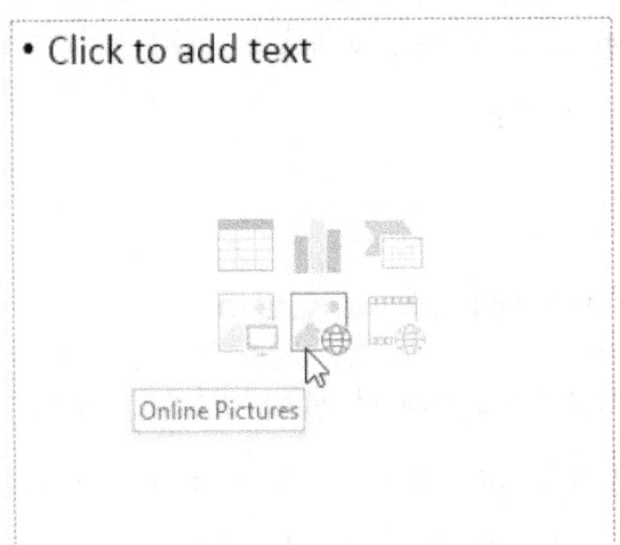

How to add video to a slide

To insert a video from a file:

- Go to the Insert tab, click on the Video drop-down arrow, then click on Video on My PC.

- Locate the desired video file, then click on Insert.

- The video will be added to the slide.

To insert an online video:

You can embed videos from sites like YouTube in your slides. The advantage of embedding is that it reduces the file size of your presentation, but internet access is needed to play the videos.

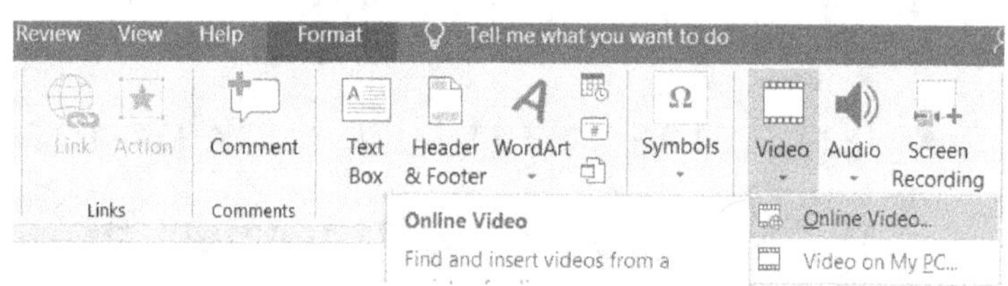

How to trim a video

- Click on the video, then go to Playback tab on the Ribbon.

- Then click on the Trim Video command.

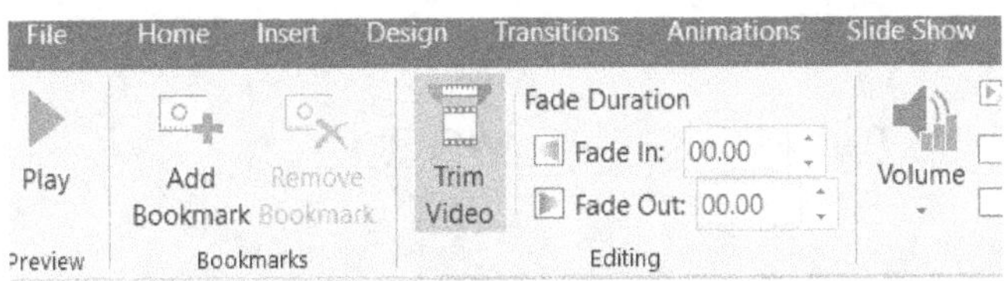

- A dialog box pops up. Use the green handle to set the start time and the red handle to set end time.

- Click the Play button to preview the video.
- Click OK when you are done trimming the video.

How to Insert audio to slide
To insert audio from a file:

- Go to the insert tab, then click on the Audio drop-down arrow, click Audio on My PC.
- Locate the desired Audio file, then click on Insert.
- The audio will be added to the slide.

To record audio:

- Go to the insert tab, then click on the Audio drop-down arrow, click Record Audio.

- Name the recording by entering a name.

- To start recording, simply click on the Record button.

- Click the stop button when done recording.

- Press the Play button to preview your recording.

- Click OK. The audio will be added to the slide.

WORKING WITH TABLES AND CHARTS

A table is often the best choice when presenting a PowerPoint slide with a lot of data, this is because tables helps present data in an organized and easy-to-read manner. Including a chart in a presentation allows your audience to see the meaning behind the numbers, which makes it easy to visualize comparisons and trends.

How to insert table on a slide

- If the slide includes a content placeholder, click on the Insert Table button.

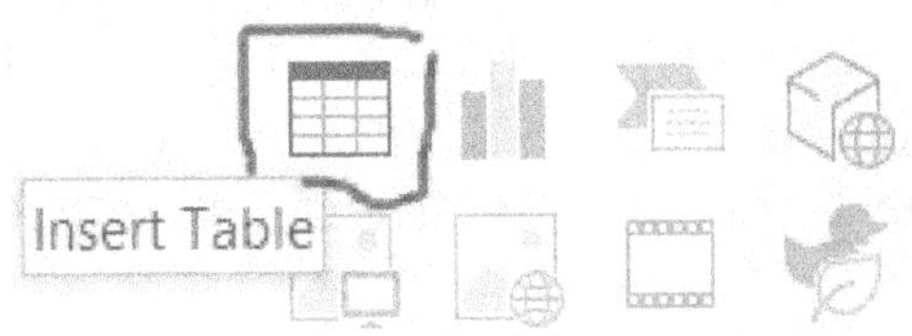

- From the Insert Table dialog box, enter the Number of column and the Number or rows, then click on the OK button.

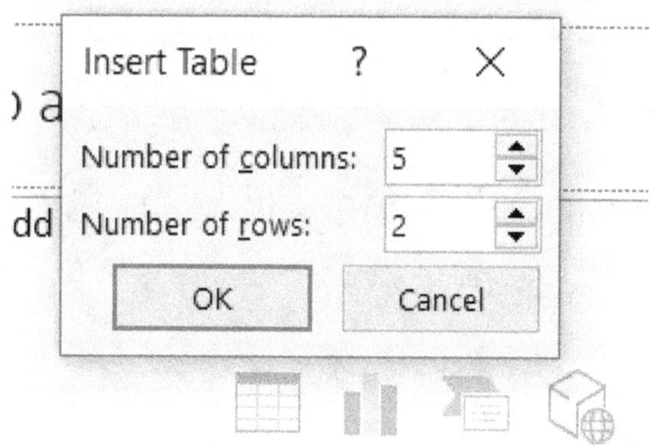

- The table is created on your slide

Note: If the context placeholder is not available, go to the **Insert Tab**, click on Table and then click on **Insert Table**.

Modify table structure

To change the size of a table

- Activate the table, and then
- Drag the sizing handles to change the height, width, or height and width of the table.

or

- Go to the Layout tool tab, in the Table Size group, set the Height or Width to a specific dimension.

To change the width of one or more columns

- Select the column or columns you want to change,, then
- Double-click the right border of a column to size the column to fit its widest content.

or

- On the Layout tool tab, in the Cell Size group, click the arrows to the right of the Width box to increase or decrease the width one unit at a time.

How to insert rows and column

To add a row above a particular row:

- First of all, select the row by simply clicking on it.
- Go to Layout table, then click on Insert Above
- A new row will be added above the selected row.

Note: By clicking the Insert Below button, a new row will be added below the selected row.

To add a column before a particular column:

- First of all, select the column by simply clicking on it.
- Go to Layout table, then click on the Insert Left button.
- A new column will be added before the selected column.

Note: By clicking the Insert Right button, a new column will be added after the selected column.

To insert a chart on a slide

- Go to the Insert tab, then click the Chart button in the Illustrations group. or click the

Insert Chart button on the content placeholder.

- In the left pane of the Insert Chart dialog box, click a chart category to display the chart variations in the right pane.

- In the right pane, click the chart type that you want to create, and then click OK to insert a sample chart and open its associated excel worksheet containing the plotted data.

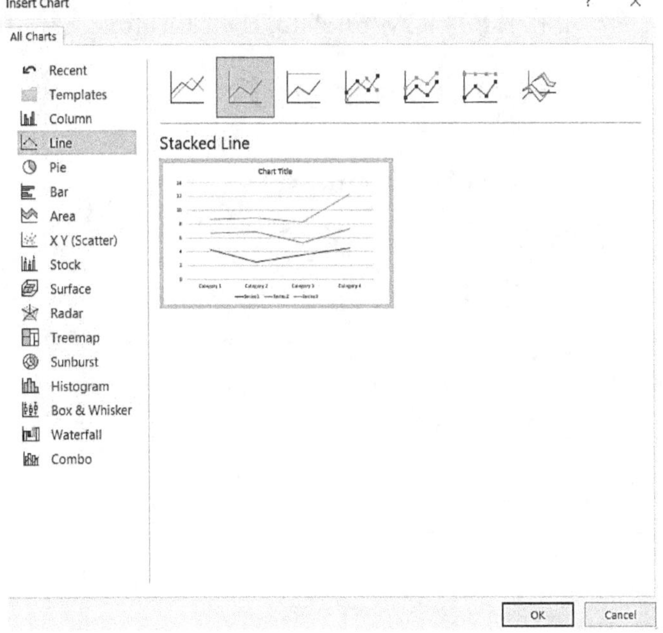

- In the linked excel worksheet, enter the values to be plotted, following the pattern of the sample data.

- If the chart data range defined by the colored outlines doesn't automatically expand to include new data, drag the blue handle in the lower-right corner of the range to expand it.

Click

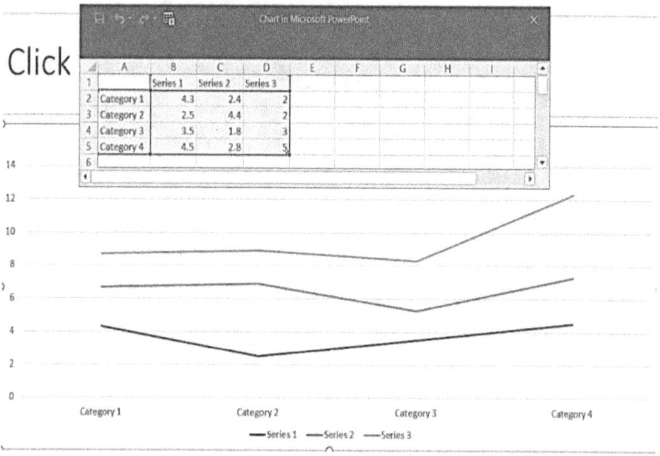

- Close the excel window when you are done.

- The chart will be completed.

How to change chart type

- Go to the Design tool tab, in the Type group, click on Change Chart Type button.

- In the Change Chart Type dialog box, click a category on the left, click a chart type at the top, and then click OK.

How to switch row and column data

- Double click on the chart you want to change. The Design tab will be displayed.
- Click on Edit Data.
- Then Click on the chart again, then click on the Switch Row/Column button.
- This switches the rows and columns.

How to change the chart layout

You can modify elements on the chart to make it easier to read.

- Double click on the chart you want to change. This makes the Design Tab appear.

- Click on the Quick Layout command.

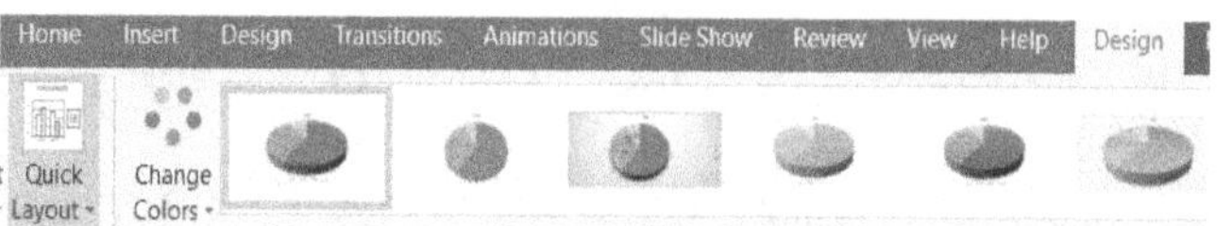

- From the menu that appears select the desired predefined layout.

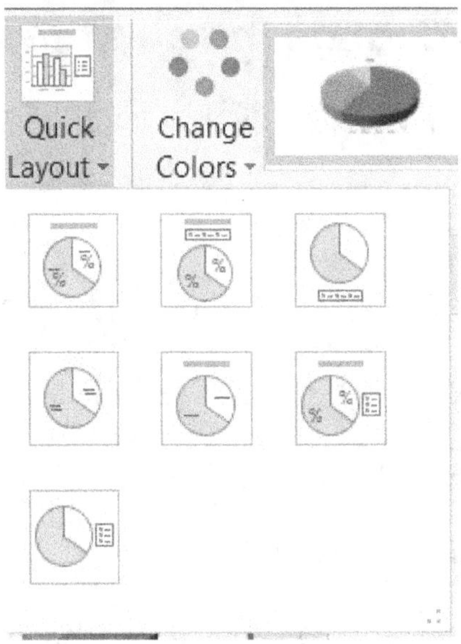

- The chart will update to reflect the new layout.

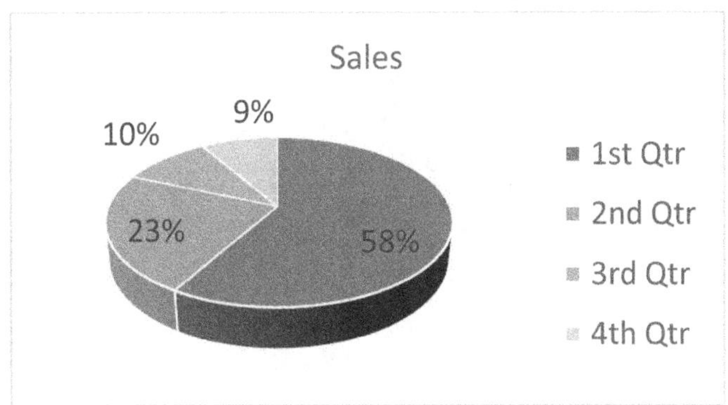

How to change the chart style

To modify the look and feel of your chart;

- Double click on the chart you want to change. This makes the Design Tab appear.
- Click on the More drop-down arrow in the Chart Styles group.
- Choose the style you prefer from the menu that appears.

USING SMARTART GRAPHICS

With SmartArt, you can communicate information with graphics instead of just text. PowerPoint presents you with a variety of styles to choose from.

How to insert a SmartArt graphic

- Go to the Insert tab, then click on SmartArt command.

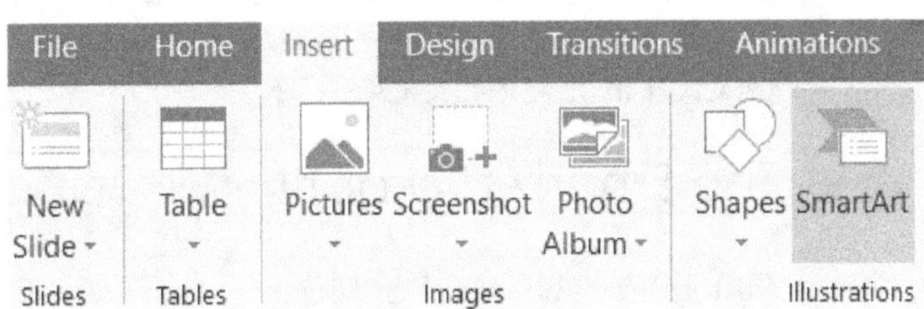

- A dialog box will appear. Select a category on the left, choose the desired SmartArt graphic, then click OK.

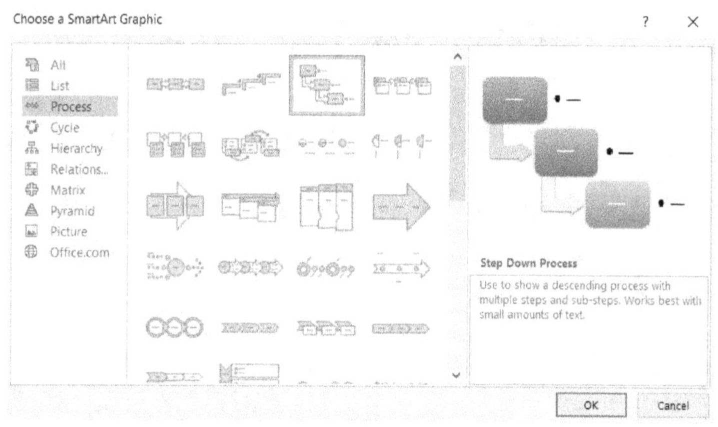

- A dialog box pops-up. Choose a category on the left, then choose your desired SmartArt graphic. Click on OK.

- The SmartArt graphic will appear on the current slide.

Tip: You can also click the Insert a SmartArt Graphic command in a placeholder to add SmartArt.

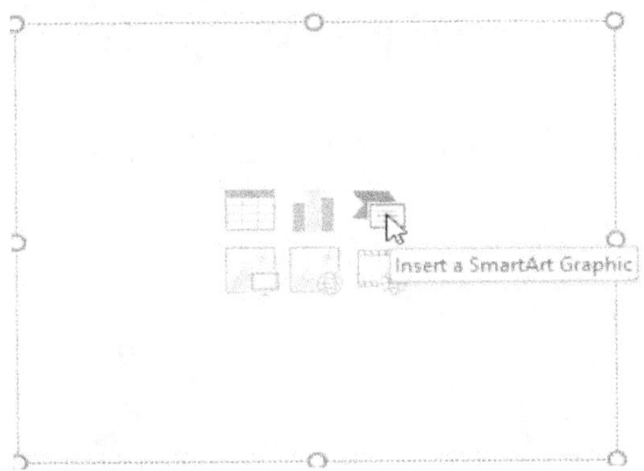

How to add text to a SmartArt graphic

- Click on the SmartArt graphic placeholder on the slide. This will make a text pane appear on the left.

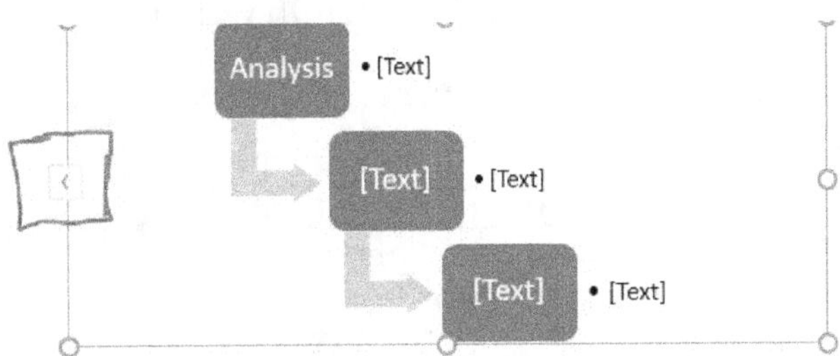

- Enter the text into each bullet on the text pane. The text will automatically appear on the corresponding shape.

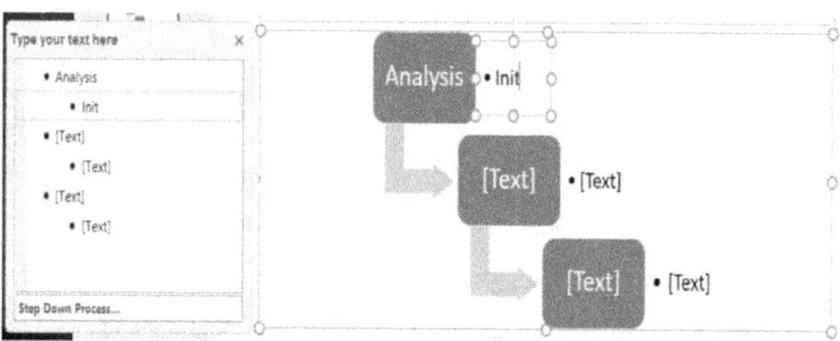

Tip: You can add text to a SmartArt graphic simply by clicking on the shape and then typing.

How to change the SmartArt layout

You can always modify the SmartArt graphic layout if the way information within it is not appealing to you.

- Double click on the SmartArt graphic you want to change. This makes the Design Tab appear.

- Click on the More drop-down arrow in the Layouts group.

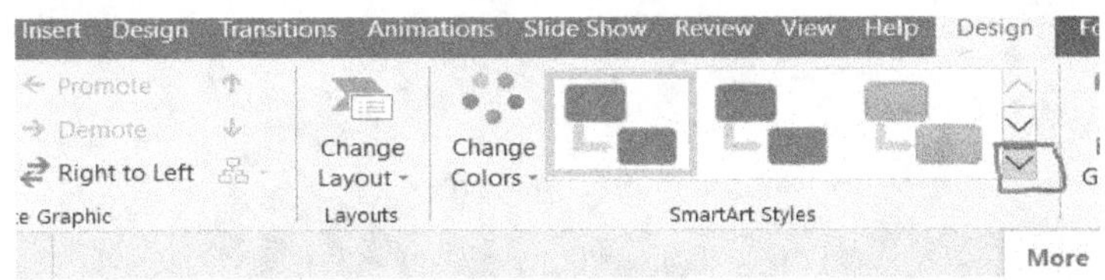

- Choose the Layout you prefer from the menu that appears.

- The slide will update to reflect the new layout.

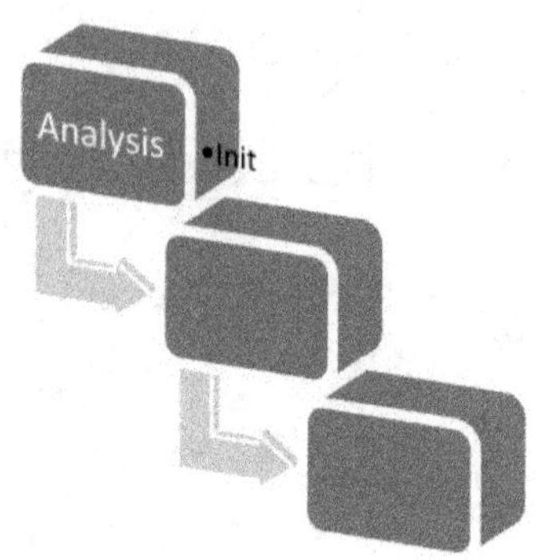

Analysis
•Init

ANIMATION EFFECTS & TRANSITIONS

Animation in PowerPoint is the way individual objects enter or exit a slide. While transition refers to the entry or exit of the entire slide as rather than the individual objects on a slide.

Animation Effects

There are four categories of animation effect that can be found in the **Animations Tab**;

Entrance: These animations control how objects enter the slide.

Emphasis: These effects animate an object that is already visible on the slide to draw attention to it, without changing its location.

Exit: These effects take an existing object through a process that results in the object no longer being visible on the slide. For example, with the Fade animation the object will simply fade away.

Motion Paths: These are similar to Emphasis effects, except the object moves within the slide along a userdefined path, like an arc.

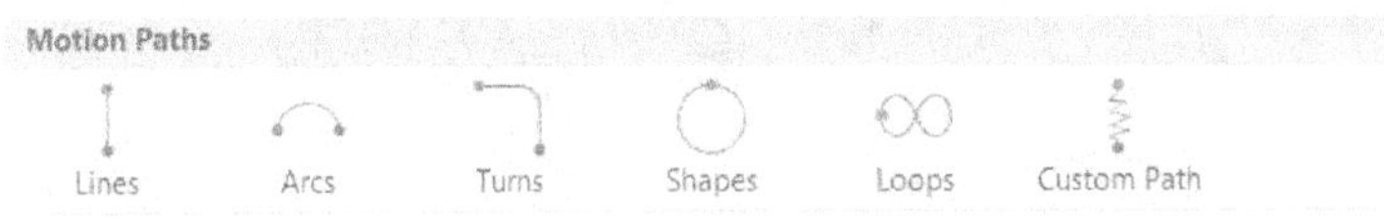

How to apply an animation to an object

- Click on the object you want to animate.

- Go to the Animations tab, then click on the More drop-down arrow.

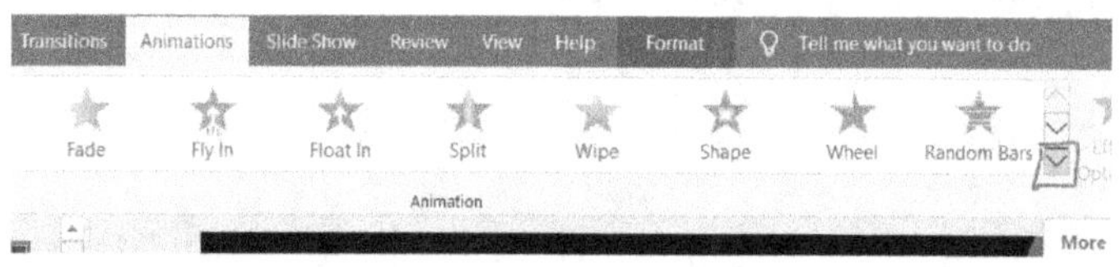

- Click on your desired effect from the drop-down menu that appears.

- The effect is applied to the object. You will see a small number next to the object. This shows that the object is animated.

Tip: You can access additional effects at the bottom of the menu.

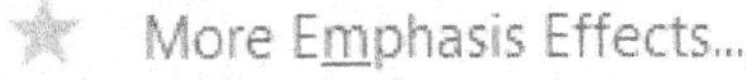

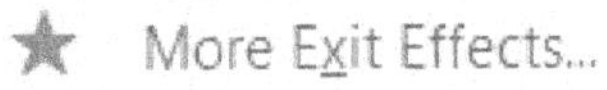

Add multiple animations to an object

- Click on the object
- Go to the Animations tab, then click on Add Animation to view the available animations.

- Then click on the animation effect you want.

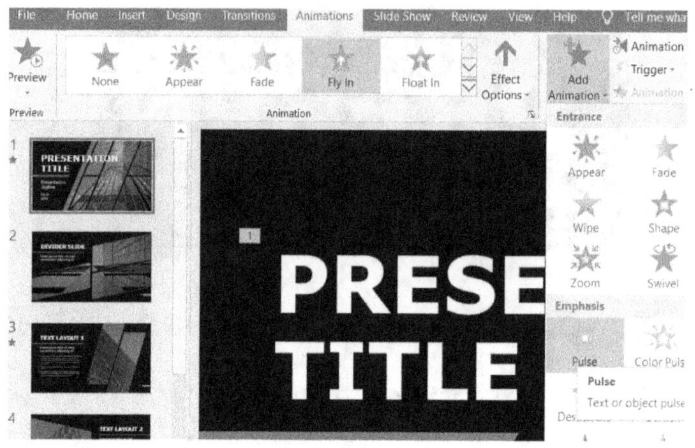

- If the object has more than one effect, it will have a different number for each effect. The numbers indicate the order in which the effects will occur.

Transitions

There are three categories of transitions that can be found in the **Transitions Tab**;

Subtle: These are basic types of transitions that use simple animations to move between slide.

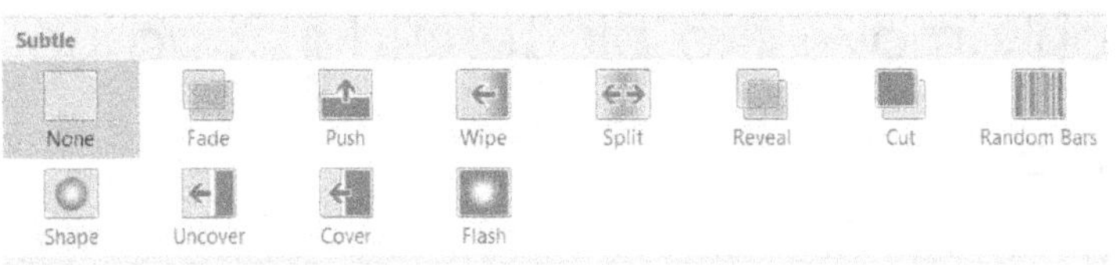

Exciting: They are more eye catching than Subtle because they use more complex animations to transition between slides. It is highly recommended not to add too many as they can make your presentation look less professional.

Dynamic Content: When transitioning between two slides that make use of similar slide layouts, this transition will only move the placeholders and not the actual slides.

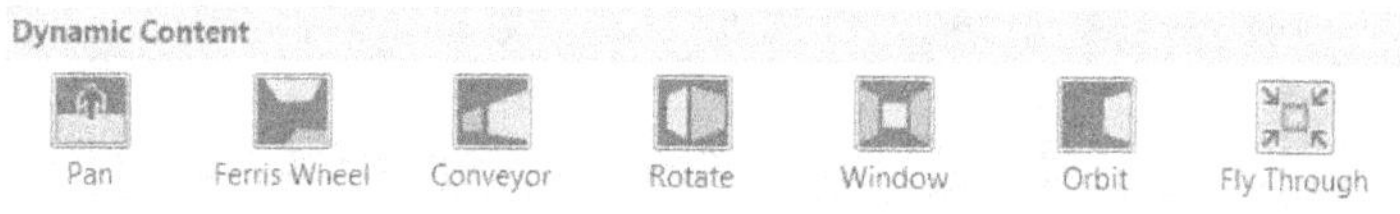

Note: Transitions should be used in moderation. Using too many transitions can make your presentation distracting. It is recommended that the subtle transition is most appropriate if you are to use a transition effect in your presentation.

How to apply a transition

- From the slide pane, select the slide that will appear after the transition.

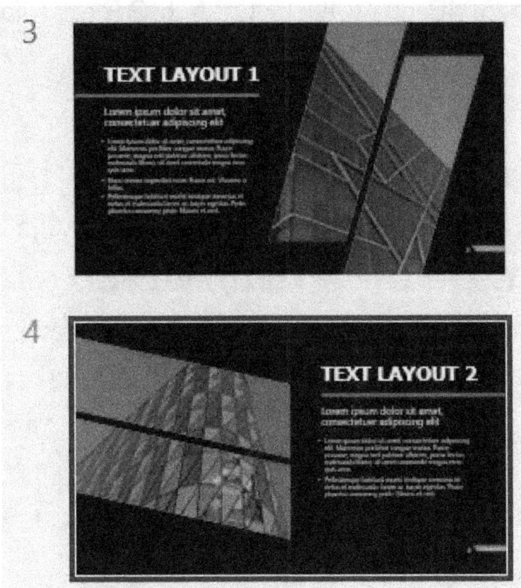

- Go to the Transitions tab, then click on the More drop-down arrow to show all transitions.

- Select a transition to apply it to the slide. This will automatically give you a slide transition preview.

Tip: To apply the chosen transition to the entire slides in your presentation, simply click on **Apply To All.**

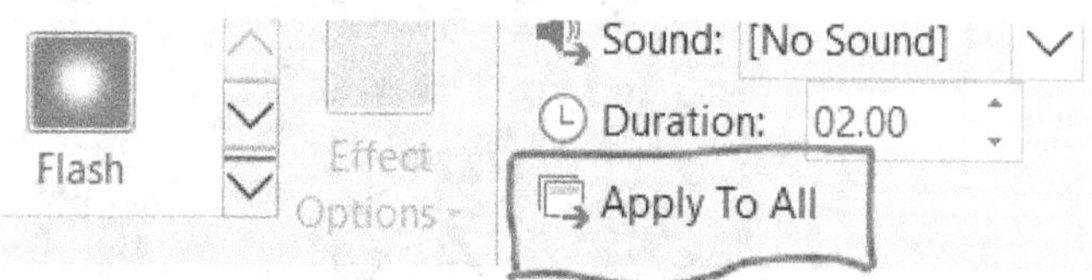

How to modify the transition effect

- Click on the slide with the transition you want to modify.

- Then go to the Transitions tab, click on Effect Options and select your preferred option. The options displayed will vary depending on the transition selected.

How to add sound to transition

- From the slide pane, click on the slide with the transition you want to add the sound effect.

- Then go to the Transitions tab, click on the Sound drop-down menu.

- Choose a sound, then click on preview to hear the sound.

How to remove a transition

- From the slide pane, click on the slide with the transition you want removed.
- Go to the Transition tab and click on None from the Transition to This Slide group.

FINALIZE PRESENTATIONS

In this chapter will guide you on how to configure slides for presentation or printing, inspecting and finalizing presentations, printing presentations and handouts.

Formatting slide for printing

There are several layouts to choose from when printing a PowerPoint presentation. The desired layout chosen by you is determined on why the slide show is been printed. PowerPoint has four types of print layouts.

Full Page Slides: A full page for each slide in your presentation is printed. This layout is best suited when you need to edit or review a printed copy of your presentation.

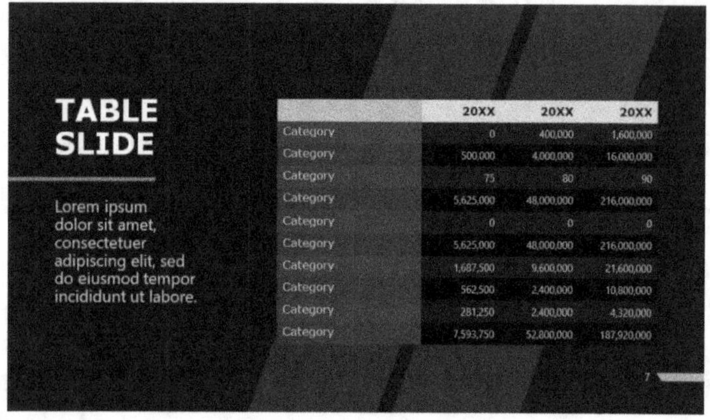

Notes Pages: The speaker notes if any is printed along with each slide.

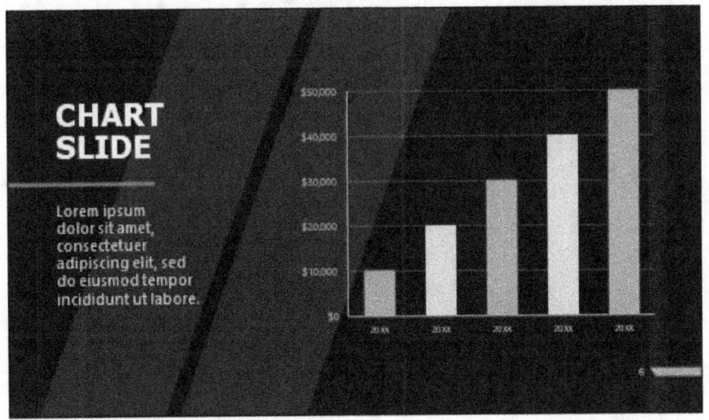

- What are the cost incurred?
- What are the factors affecting sales?
- What is the estimated growth?

Outline: The overall outline of the slide show is printed. This is most useful when you need to review the organization of your slide show.

1 PRESENTATION
TITLE
1 Presentation
Tagline
2 Month
3 20XX

2 DIVIDER SLIDE
Lorem ipsum dolor sit amet, consectetuer adipiscing elit

3 TEXT LAYOUT 1
1 Lorem ipsum dolor sit amet, consectetuer adipiscing elit
2 •Lorem ipsum dolor sit amet, consectetuer adipiscing elit. Maecenas porttitor congue massa. Fusce posuere, magna sed pulvinar ultricies, purus lectus malesuada libero, sit amet commodo magna eros quis urna.
•Nunc viverra imperdiet enim. Fusce est. Vivamus a tellus.
•Pellentesque habitant morbi tristique senectus et netus et malesuada fames ac turpis egestas. Proin pharetra nonummy pede. Mauris et orci.

4 TEXT LAYOUT 2
1 Lorem ipsum dolor sit amet, consectetuer adipiscing elit
2 •Lorem ipsum dolor sit amet, consectetuer adipiscing elit. Maecenas porttitor congue massa. Fusce posuere, magna sed pulvinar ultricies, purus lectus malesuada libero, sit amet commodo magna eros quis urna.
•Pellentesque habitant morbi tristique senectus et netus et malesuada fames ac turpis egestas. Proin pharetra nonummy pede. Mauris et orci.

5 COMPARISON
1 Section 1 Title

Handouts: The thumbnail versions of each slide is printed. It also has an optional space for notes. This layout is suited for instances where you want to give your audience a physical copy of your presentation. The optional space is for them to take notes on each slide.

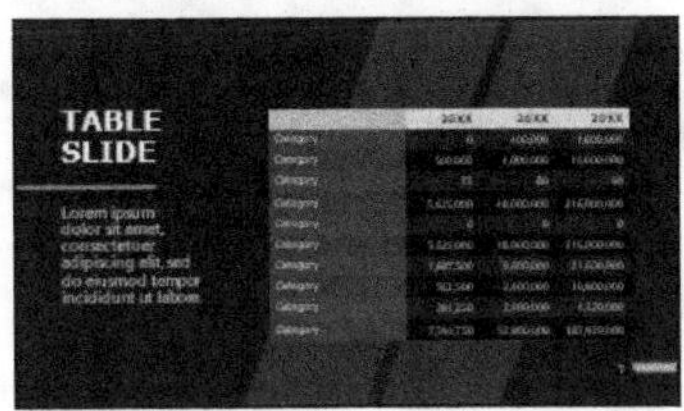

How to print a presentation

- Click on the File tab.

- Then click on Print from the Backstage view that appears.

- The Print pane will appear. Then select your printer.

- Proceed further by choosing your desired print layout and color settings.

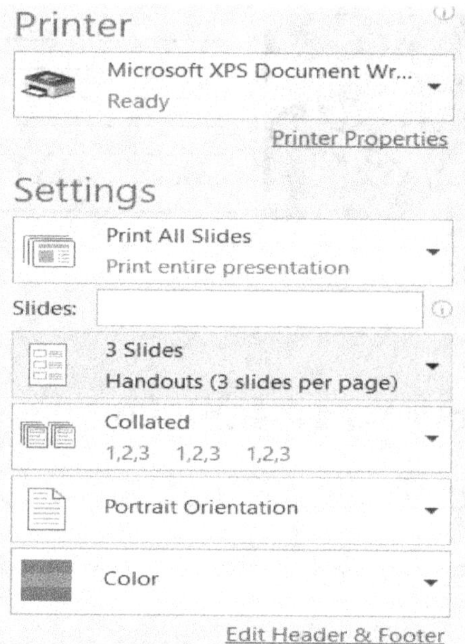

- Click on Print.

Print

How to start a slide show

You can start your presentation using different ways:

✓ On the **Quick Access Toolbar**, click on Start From Beginning command, or press the F5 key on your keyboard. This will make the presentation appear in full-screen mode.

✓ Alternatively, click on the Slide show view button at the bottom of the PowerPoint screen to begin the slide show from the current slide.

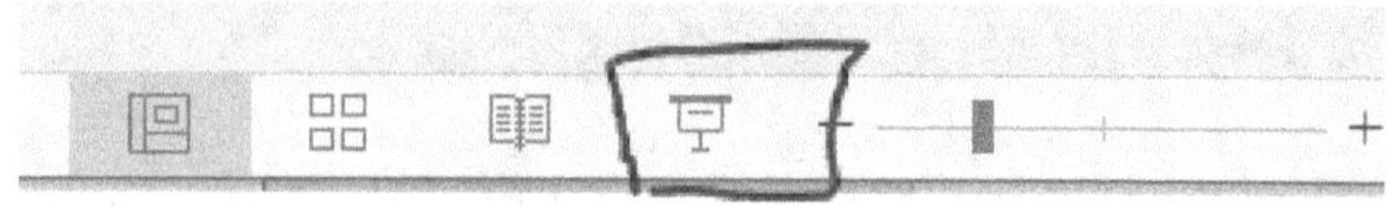

✓ Or go to the Slide Show tab, you can start the presentation from the beginning or from current slide. You are also presented with other advanced presentation options.

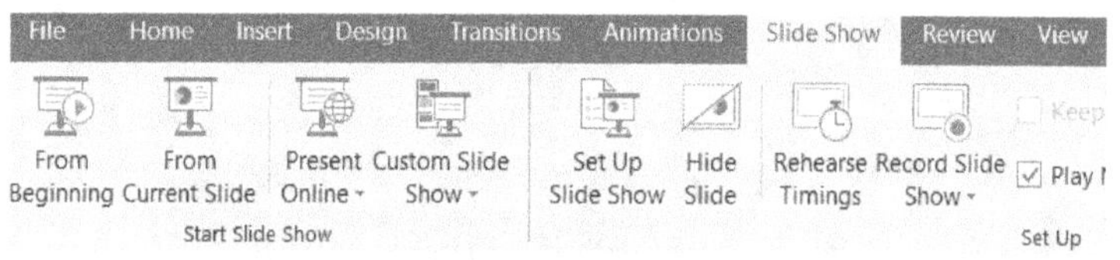

How to access Presenter view

If you are using a projector to present your slide, the Presenter view should be used. With the Presenter view, you get access to special set of controls on your screen that won't be visible to your audience. With the Presenter view you will get access to reference slide notes, preview the next coming slide and a lot more.

To access the presenters view, simply press **Alt + F5** on your keyboard.

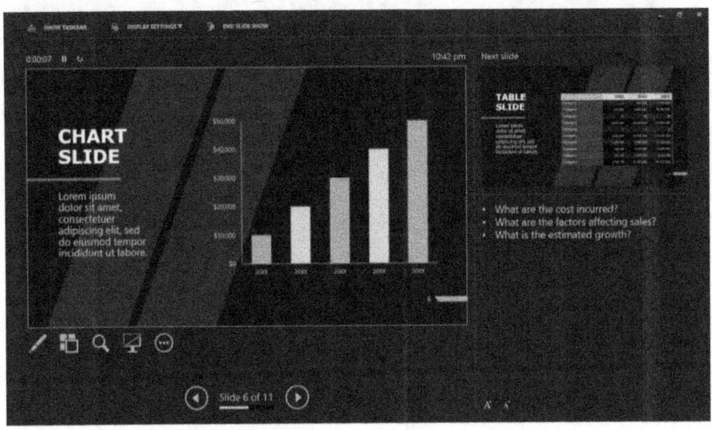

Adding narration to a presentation

- Go to the **Slide Show** tab, click on the Record Slide Show drop-down arrow, then click on either **Start Recording from Beginning** or **Start Recording from Current Slide**.

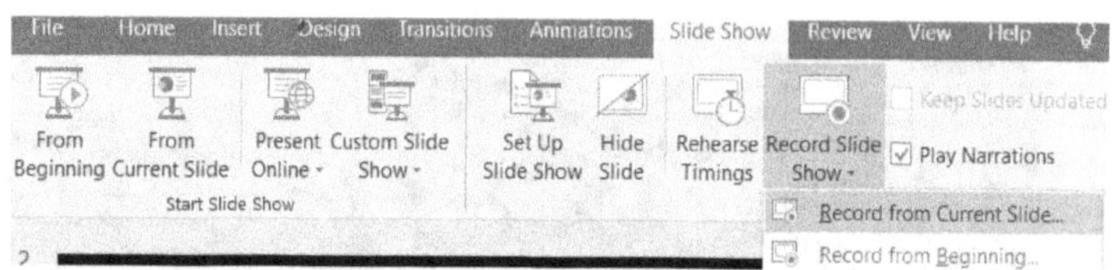

- Then click on **Start Recording** from the dialog box that appears. It should be noted that you can only record a narration if there is a microphone attached to your PC or your computer has an inbuilt microphone.

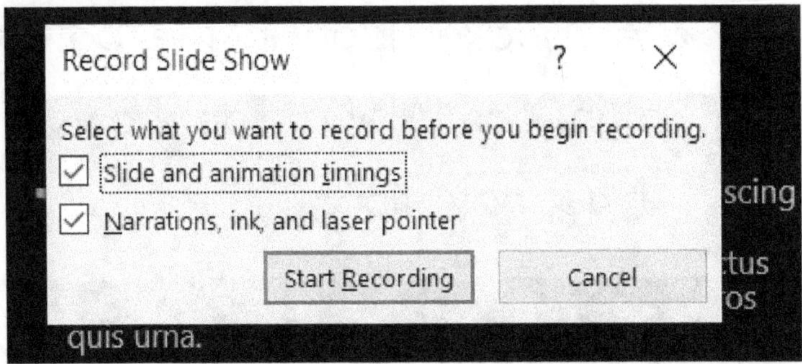

- Your presentation will be displayed in full-screen view. ensure to speak clearly into the microphone.

- Click on the Next button on the Recording toolbar to move to the next slide.

- PowerPoint will close the full-screen view when you get to the end of the show.

- A speaker icon in the bottom-right corner of a slide shows that it has narration.

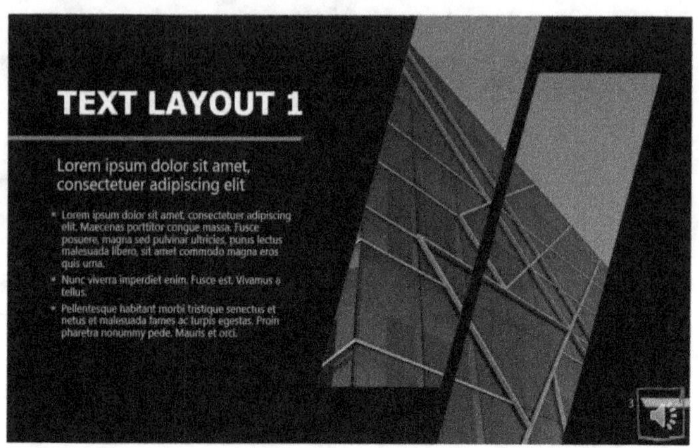

Tip: When you record a slide show, the mouse pointer is not visible in the final product, therefore, if you want to draw someone's attention to a detail you need to make use of the laser pointer or pen tool feature. To do this, click pen icon that is found on the bottom of the screen while you are recording.

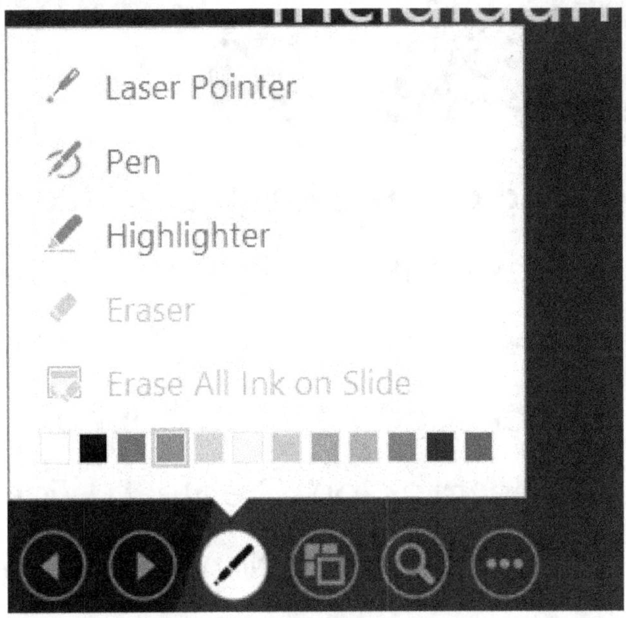

How to remove narration

Go to the Slide Show tab, then click on the Record SLide Show drop-down arrow. Then hover the mouse over clear, then click on the option you want from the menu.

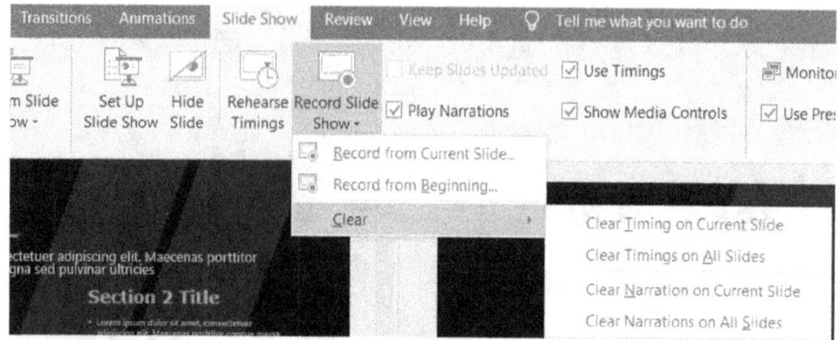

Exporting a presentation as a video

- Click on the File tab.

- Then click on Export from the Backstage view that appears.

- Then click on Create a Video. Video export options will appear on the right.

- You can select the Presentation Quality by clicking on the drop-down arrow.

- Click Create Video.

- From the Save As dialog box, navigate the location where you want to save the presentation, then enter presentation name.

- Click Save.

Other Books by the Author

APPLE WATCH
SERIES 5
USER'S GUIDE

The Complete Beginners Guide to Mastering
Your iWatch Series 5

THOMAS JACKSON

www.ingramcontent.com/pod-product-compliance
Lightning Source LLC
Chambersburg PA
CBHW071526150726
48000CB00002B/709